The Woman in the Now

From the **Crack Pipe** and **Prostitution** *to* the **Pulpit**

Stephanie Gamble

This book is a work of non-fiction. All details are true and accurate according to the author's memory.

Published by CLF PUBLISHING, LLC. 3281 E. Guasti Road, Seventh Floor, Ontario, CA 91761. (760) 669-8149.

Copyright © 2013 by Stephanie Gamble. All rights reserved. No portion of this book may be reproduced, stored in a retrieval system, or transmitted by any form or any means electronically, photocopied, recorded, or any other except for brief quotations in printed reviews, without the prior permission of the publisher.

Cover Design by Senior Design. Contact information- info@senirdesign.com.

ISBN # 978-0-9857372-7-6

Printed in the United States of America.

Acknowledgements

First and foremost, I acknowledge my Lord and Savior Jesus Christ, who is my deliverer, my healer, my keeper, my strength, and my everything.

To my angel, my mother who is deceased and who prayed me through. The bible says the prayers of the righteous availeth much. I thank my mom for praying for me through my addiction. Even though I know it hurt her to see me strung out, she prayed me through. If it had not been for her prayers, I doubt I would have made it. So, I dedicate this book to my mom.

To my husband Demetrius for falling in love with me in my addiction and for not judging me and knowing we were meant to be soul mates. Thank you honey, for following your heart and the Spirit of the Living God.

To my sister Rosalind and brother-in-law Charles Travis for being my guardian angels and for putting up with me, my mess and my addiction, for opening up their doors when I became homeless, and for being led by the Spirit to be a great part of my testimony.

To my niece Rhanesha (Rah-rah) for always accepting me when I was rejected by many. She kept a smile on my heart, and she gave me hope.

To my sister Lisa for understanding.

To my sister Yolanda for not knowing the unknown.

My armor bearer and friend Tahtia Kidd, for pushing me to write my book. Thanks, T.

Table of Contents

Introduction		7
Chapter 1	How It All Started	9
Chapter 2	Bored	11
Chapter 3	Curious	13
Chapter 4	Blasted	15
Chapter 5	Party Time (So I thought)!	17
Chapter 6	The Cost	19
Chapter 7	Getting Twisted	21
Chapter 8	Loose as a Goose, but Covered	23
Chapter 9	Wild N' Out	25
Chapter 10	It was Judas, not Boaz	27
Chapter 11	My Boaz	29
Chapter 12	The Relapse	33
Chapter 13	Same Game, Different Location	35
Chapter 14	Never Say Never	37
Chapter 15	Moving on, or So I Thought	39
Chapter 16	Getting Scandalous	41

Chapter 17	*Anything and Everything*	43
Chapter 18	*Delusional*	45
Chapter 19	*Snitches*	47
Chapter 20	*Didn't Want to Live Anymore*	49
Chapter 21	*The Visitation*	53
Chapter 22	*Going to my Father's House*	57
Chapter 23	*Delivered*	59
Chapter 24	*More than a Conqueror*	61

Definitions	64
Scriptures	66
About the Author	69
A Message from the Author	71

Introduction

The primary purpose of this book of the story of my life is to let my readers know God can do anything but fail! God specializes in impossibilities. All things are possible through Christ Jesus. If you (or someone you know) are struggling with an addiction of any sort, the addiction doesn't have to be drugs, it could be women, men, lying, cheating, stealing, alcohol, gambling, jealousy, envy, money, sex, and abuse, this book is for you. I am a living witness that God can deliver you (bring you out) from anything. Nothing is too hard for God; if God did it for me, He can do it for you or a loved one.

I pray this book gives you hope because there is hope. I double dare you to follow the instructions of Jeremiah 29:11-14. This is my story; this is my song; I am praising my savior all the day long!

At the end of each chapter, I added a note page to inspire you to write down your thoughts. Write down anything that the spirit is saying to you as you read the story of my life. You may even write a scripture that comes to mind.

To God be the glory forever. Amen!

Stephanie Gamble

Chapter 1

How It All Started: The Plan, the Plot

On the way home from school one day, I ran into an old close friend from elementary school. My friend looked as if she was not doing well, and I decided to lend a helping hand. I helped her catch up with housecleaning, laundry, and dinner for the kids. I left school early one day to help my best friend again, and before I could knock on the door, she burst through it. I asked her, "What is wrong?" She replied, "Girl, I have something I want you to try." (Satan was using my best friend.) She went into the bedroom where her husband usually stayed. I heard fast talking, dealing, and a lot of whispering. (This was the plot: they were going to get me hooked on crack. I had enough jewelry on my neck for them to smoke all night.)

My friend came out with a micro dot looking substance, and I asked her, "What is that tiny little thing?" She told me it was 'free base' rock cocaine. (The first hit is free.) She pulled out a glass tube called a base pipe, put the substance in the tube, and lit the pipe. Trusting her, I wasn't thinking when I followed her directions to "just pull."

That "pull" changed my life and took me to places I never thought I would go. With that one "pull," I entered into a world of darkness, a world with no limits, not knowing I was getting ready to become strung out on drugs from a prostitute, to becoming a strawberry (sex for drugs), to committing robbery and burglary. I was gang raped, a stripper, had physical sickness, an encounter with a serial killer, experienced anger, depression, denial, and hopelessness. I was all the way to the point of suicide. I was arrested twenty-seven times and was going back and forth to prison.

Notes

_____

_____

_____

_____

_____

_____

_____

_____

_____

Chapter 2

Bored

(One month later)

One sunny day, I was sitting on my porch. I was bored and looking up and down the street. I was very bored. The Bible tells me that an idle mind is the devil's workshop. One thing I do know is if you let the devil ride, before you know it, he will drive. I began to walk back and forth to the corner of 65th Street and Denver in L.A., California. I always saw a lot of cars and women walking. They were getting in and out of different cars.

I asked myself, 'What is going on around this corner?' I soon found out it was a dope house! So, I stood on the corner the next day curious about what was going on with the girls and the cars. I later found out the girls were prostitutes and the dope dealer was their pimp.

Notes

_____

_____

_____

Stephanie Gamble

Chapter 3

Curious

I was standing on the corner one day, watching all the excitement of the cars and the women going back and forth when a blue Mercedes hit that corner and stopped. The driver rolled down his window and looked at me and said, "Damn! Hey, Cutie!" I had no idea he was the owner of the dope spot and the pimp of the prostitutes!

He told me to go on down to the little white house, so he could get to know me better. So, I walked. I walked down to that little white house, and a short, dark skinned, skinny man got out of the blue Mercedes and introduced himself as Mr. Dean. He told me the white house was his spot and the girls I saw were his girls. I was in awe! He said, "Come on in."

I went into his house. There were about nine ladies sitting, purchasing drugs, changing clothes, leaving out the door, and getting into cars that were waiting outside. We exchanged words; then, he put a hit on a pipe and passed it to me. I remembered this was the same thing my friend offered to me when I went to help her clean up. So I took it, and he lit up the pipe for me and said the same exact words she did: "Just pull." I did, and he gave me a couple more hits, just enough to get me "sprung." He wanted to see my reaction- whether or not I would want more.

After sitting for two hours wanting more, a prostitute named Breezy walked in. She was loud, funny, and cute. She had a hand full of money, almost one thousand dollars. She gave it to the pimp in exchange for a package the size of a golf ball. She looked at me at that moment and asked, "Who is this cutie?" Then, she broke a piece off the golf-ball sized package about the size of a button. I soon found out it wasn't just a hit but what they called a 'blast'! She lit it and hit it first. Then, she passed it to me and said the same thing, "'Pull' Mama." When I let up off the pipe, I couldn't see, talk, or move. I was blasted. Mind you, this wasn't the first time I had heard the word 'pull.' Three times, you're out.

Notes

_____
_____
_____
_____
_____
_____
_____

Chapter 4

Blasted

When Breezy got up to leave, she looked back at me and said, "Come on, Mama. Go with me." I had no idea what I was getting myself into. We got into a car, a 'trick's car' is what she called it. She didn't really know how to drive, so she asked me if I knew how to drive. I answered, "Yes." She pulled over and said, "Drive B***h" and started laughing right off the top. I liked her style; she was very funny to me. I asked her where we were going, and she told me, "To get more dope and money." I was very excited! Remember, I was already sprung, so this sounded really good to me. We ended up going to the Hoover Crips' hood. When she got out, all the gang bangers started calling her name because they knew she kept money; she was what they called 'a real hoe.'

She was a pickpocket thief and anything but a flat backer (someone who just lies down and has sex for money). She, in other words, took what she wanted, living very dangerously. She bought more dope; then, she jumped in the car and said, "Let's roll." We went to the motel where a man (trick) had been waiting for over five hours to buy sex when she had told him she would be right back. When you are sprung, you'll do just about anything- even lend a prostitute your car while you're in a motel for hours, hoping she will come back. We ended up going to the motel. The man didn't care how long she had been gone just as long as she had dope when she got back. He didn't even ask where she had been. He said, "Did you get anything?" Isn't that something? She ended up getting dressed as the trick smoked. She gave me an outfit, some heels, and a long wig to put on. Little did I know I was being tricked (turned out) into becoming a prostitute.

Notes

Chapter 5

Party Time (So I thought)!

We hit the boulevard, and she told me to catch a trick (a man that pays for women) and meet her back at the motel. We did this for the next six months, and to me, it became a way to support my habit and have a party every day! We were very tight. By that time, we were best friends. I had become a prostitute overnight, and I liked it.

Partying all day every day, I started meeting all kinds of ladies of the night and all kinds of men. I met young men, married men, single men, pimps, players, macks, gang bangers, and gangsters. They were all tricks: businessmen, men with degrees, doctors, dentists, and football players. This went on for a year; even the dope dealer became a trick.

It had gotten to the point where the money became slow. Us girls that were supporting our habit started going to the dope spots turning dates with the dope man. This was called being a 'strawberry.' A 'strawberry' is considered a very low name. Sometimes, we would trade sex for a $5 hit!

Notes

Chapter 6

The Cost

I went to jail for the first time in 1986, for prostitution; I was sentenced to thirty days. The next time I was busted for prostitution, I was sentenced to sixty days, and finally, I was sentenced to ninety days for prostitution. When I got busted again, it was for selling a controlled substance; I was sentenced to 120 days in the state dorm. Sybil Brand had become a home for me.

All the prostitutes would end up there at the same time, so it made jail fun because I knew almost everyone there. We would make the best of it, and our men would come see us and put a hot forty dollars on our books every day. At that time, I was going with a big dope dealer named Lionel. So, some of us were ballers in jail, meaning we were 'running things' because we were able to have a commissary: big stores with candy, cigarettes, and hot coffee. Commissary came twice a week. All the other days and weekends, I was making money. That's really against the law. One specific time, my real sister Lisa and I were both in there because I was scandalous and used her name Alethia Hatcher, because the judge told me the next time I got busted, I would go to prison.

Notes

Chapter 7

Getting Twisted

One day, I got busted with a .357 Magnum that my boyfriend made me carry because of the lifestyle. Some guys tried to jack me because by that time I had started smoking and selling my own product. And the game always said, "Don't smoke your own product. It leads to destruction." And that's what it did.

Things started to get worse because I ended up smoking most, if not all, of my product. So, I started turning dates with high rolling dope dealers like Freeway Rick & The Freeway Boys, Third World, and Whities Enterprise. I would get anything from a quarter piece to a half ounce for a date. I became strung out! This went on for another five years.

Notes

_____

_____

_____

_____

Stephanie Gamble

Chapter 8

Loose as a Goose, but Covered

At that time, HIV was spreading rapidly. I had six or seven friends who were infected with the disease. They all ended up sick and passed away. I know God made death behave. These were people who I had sexual encounters with, so I know that I know, that I know, God had His hand on me. Thank you, Jesus! Around this time, a serial killer named DT was killing girls left and right, between Imperial and Vernon on Figueroa. Unfortunately, I lost six girlfriends in the murders. We all worked Figueroa. I remember getting into a car with the serial killer D.T, but by the grace of God, it wasn't my time to go, and it wasn't his time to kill. Jeremiah 29:11 says, *"For I know the plans I have towards you."* So by the grace of God, I escaped death.

Notes

_____

_____

_____

Stephanie Gamble

Chapter 9

Wild N' Out

I got busted while I was on parole in another dope house with twenty rocks on me and was sentenced to three years in prison. By God's grace, I did half my time. When I went home, I started smoking crack again while I was on parole. It had become so bad; I knew by then I needed some real help. My life was going down the drain real fast once again. I went into the drug program by my mother's request. That same day, my friend Jazzy and my boyfriend Lionel came and broke me out. As soon as I got into the car, they fixed me a hit of cocaine. I was a disappointment to my entire family. I went right back to the crack and prostitution lifestyle. I ended up getting pulled over and busted with a .357 Magnum in the car, and because I was on parole, I was sentenced to twelve months in the state penitentiary: CCWF. Upon my release, I went right back to smoking and prostitution, for another ten years.

Notes

Chapter 10

It was Judas, not Boaz

My relationship with Lionel was very abusive; he would jump on me and beat me up. He became a closet smoker himself. You know you can't hang around whores and dope (the fast life) without getting turned out. So this is what happened. Lionel started smoking too. But he didn't want anyone to know, especially his homeboys. So, he would send me to his dope spot to get ounces at a time while he was at home stuck and sprung. His workers would ask me where he was. I would have to lie and say he was at home sick. They would laugh and say, "Tell that nigga he's smoking." They were right. So, Lionel took his addiction out on me, and I had to suffer abuse because he got hooked. Well, the money didn't stop coming and neither did the whores.

Lionel and I got married while I was addicted. He had always told me I was bought and paid for, meaning if he couldn't have me no one could. I got high all night long on the day and night before my wedding, up until the time to put on my wedding dress. It was me, my sister, and a so-called friend. A real friend would have said, "You need to go to sleep because you are getting married tomorrow." Lionel spent over $3000; the wedding was nice. But the bride, me, was a mess. We continued in our hustling lifestyle for some years, until one day Lionel's dope spot got jacked, and he ended up killing the dude and got life in prison. Lionel died while in prison (R.I.P). My girlfriend Breezy was in drug rehab at the time when she asked me if I wanted to meet a clean and sober young man. I told her, "Yes." She then introduced me to Demetrius.

Notes

Chapter 11

My Boaz

In 1991, Demetrius was in a 12-step program, so I had to be very careful to make sure he did not relapse. He would come visit me on the bus every day. I was living with my mom; she gave me another chance to get it right. We watched movies, and he courted me. But as soon as he would leave, I would go and get a hit then go back home. This lasted a while, until one day he came over, and my mom told him she hadn't seen me in three days. So, he started looking around asking if anybody had seen me; he called my baby sister Lisa, and she said, "Go down on Figueroa in the 90's, and you'll find her." He did just that and found me and asked me why I had been avoiding him. I told him I didn't want to jeopardize his sobriety. He said I was really trippin' and to please just go home. I told him my mother was tired of my lies. I had good intentions, but my flesh wasn't finished. "The Spirit is willing, but the flesh is weak."

Demetrius was trying to get his life together after spending ten years of living on Skid Row. He was a nice guy and just my speed, but sin was still in my life due to drugs, alcohol, and a lack of Jesus. I was jeopardizing his sobriety. After a month of separation, he returned still to find me in worse condition than I was in before. He liked me for me and felt I could overcome this problem. He supported my habit thinking he was helping, but it didn't work.

In 1997, we got married, after having lived in sin, while Demetrius was fighting a case out of state. One day, Demetrius relapsed. After being strung out on drugs together, we hit rock bottom. We were on a mission for Satan. God came in and did a miraculous separation. My husband went to jail- facing life in prison and received a five-to-fifteen year prison sentence. I was left all alone I thought, but this was the part of life where my deliverance took place.

Notes

Stephanie Gamble

Chapter 12

The Relapse

I ended up going into the drug program again for three months and ended up getting kicked out for relapsing. I then moved into a sober-living home. I relapsed again after being there for two months.

Demetrius came to pick me up to go see my mom in the hospital. Ten minutes after we left, my mother passed away, on August 18, 1996. When I went back to the drug program, I called the hospital to see if my mother was asleep. They informed me ten minutes after I left, she expired. At the time, I didn't know what they meant when they used the term "expired." I asked, "What do you mean, she expired?" They told me, "Ma'am, she passed away." I went bizerk and went on a smoking spree.

I started feeling all alone and very confused about life. I felt as if I had no purpose to live now that my mother was gone. I lived to get high and got high to live. I ended up getting put out of sober living. The day before I left, I got a visit from my older sister Rosalind and her boyfriend Chubby who lived in Victorville. My sister looked at me in sorrow and said, "Steph, you look lost and lonely. Why don't you come to Victorville to live with us? You can start a new life there." At that time, I was willing to try just about anything. So, I asked Demetrius what I should do. He told me to move out there; I got mad at him. I thought he was trying to get rid of me, but really he wanted me to get my life together. So, I packed my things, and they came to get me the following day. I got into the car without looking back. I knew it would be the last time I saw L.A. for a while.

Notes

Chapter 13

Same Game, Different Location

I ended up falling asleep, and when I awoke, we were getting off the freeway in a little city called Victorville. I looked around and thought, *'Wow, is this it?'* I already felt I was in a dry and deserted place, and there I was moving into a dry and deserted place, but little did I know this would be my 'Victoryville.'

The bible states, *"The steps of a good man are ordered by God!"* This was to be my place of deliverance. But after being there for only a month, the devil himself knocked on my door. I opened the door and let him in again! I needed a job real bad, and I wanted it right then! I began to ask questions about strip clubs, which is the fastest way to make money. My niece Nene had friends who stripped in clubs. So, I found out where to go.

Notes

_____

_____

_____

Stephanie Gamble

Chapter 14

Never Say Never

I began working as an exotic dancer and doing pole dancing at a low-budget club called *G-Spot*. It was another way to hustle. I needed cash. My idea was to start stripping to make money to get my own place and also to make my boyfriend Demetrius mad enough to move up there with me. To my surprise, he did just that. He didn't believe I was in the club dancing, and at that time, he had become a big dope dealer. I told him, "You've been selling all this dope making all this money and you can't get me a place of my own? Oh well, I'll start dancing."

So one night, he called my sister and asked where I was. She told him I was working. He asked where exactly was I working, and she told him at a club as an exotic dancing. He told her not to tell me that he was five minutes away. He wanted Rosalind to take him to the club. She called me at the club and told me everything he had said. I said, "Good! Now, he can see that I am serious."

By the time they got there, I was finished dancing. She walked in and said he was outside and to go out there before he came in. So I walked out, and he said,

"Let's go." I said, "Do you have that money for my condo?" He said, "Let's go." When we got back to my sister's house, he handed me $3500. I looked at him and said, "Thanks, baby."

Notes

Chapter 15

Moving on, or So I Thought

I moved on, or should I say we moved on: Demetrius and I that is. We moved into a very nice two-bedroom condo on Apple Valley Rd. Dee started transporting drugs from L.A. to Victorville to Vegas. Every time he came home, he would bring out a scale and a lot of dope. He would cook it and package it right in my face. I couldn't stop it. I wanted to, but the influence was all around me. When he left again, he called it going to work, so I left too.

I didn't know that much about Victorville, but I still got in my car. I went to the gas station and sat there until I saw somebody that looked like she knew about the 'game'- the drug game that is. A girl walked up, and I asked, "Hey, where is the happenings around here?" She asked me what I was looking for. "Where do they get high around here?" She pointed and said, "All around here. Downtown on D Street." So, I went and parked in the lot across from the Green Spot Motel. That became my every day spot. I ended up turning a few girls out. I was starting a prostitution ring in Victorville, where it was normally a quite small little town. Everything I left in L.A., I brought up to Victorville and started all over again.

Notes

Chapter 16

Getting Scandalous

Meanwhile, Demetrius was still transporting drugs from L.A. to Las Vegas and never coming home. He would just stop on the way to Las Vegas to cook his dope and package it up, which gave me the opportunity to collect all the crumbs and ask him to leave me an ounce or two to sell here in Victorville. As soon as he left, I would hit the downtown Victorville area to sell, smoke, and party all day every day. It had become a hustling life for me all over again! I kept drugs on me all the time because my man was the dope man. I would smoke up all the dope then turn around and spend all the money I made on more dope to smoke. Then, I began to sell our property: guns, jewelry, marijuana, coats, and shoes, practically anything I could sell to get dope. Then, I began to start stealing everything that wasn't bolted down.

We started going into Food 4 Less. We would grab a shopping cart and fill it up with items we knew dope dealers needed: diapers, meats, hygiene, but most of all liquor. We got a fifth of everything. Once the basket was overflowing, we would then push it right out of the back door. We did this every day until their inventory grew very short. They waited on us to make our move one day and chased us out the store. Food 4 Less ended up putting a T.V. camera at its back door because of us.

Notes

Chapter 17

Anything and Everything

I did so many things that I said I would never do- so many belittling scandalous things. I remember STDs were running rampant in the nineties, and there I was having unprotected sex. Yes, I contracted most of them, but by the grace of God, no weapon formed against me shall prosper. God had His hand on me the whole time. Smoking crack is no joke. The saying is, "crack kills," and you better believe it because it will. And I did just about anything and everything to get that next hit! And when I couldn't get crack, I tried any and everything else that was on the streets.

I pumped poison into my body for twenty long years. I smoked "Angel Dust," which is embalming fluid. It is what is inserted into dead people to swell them up in their caskets. I tried Sherman & Lovely, which is a part of the Angel Dust family. I've tried L.S.D., Acid, Heroin, Pills, Mushrooms, and liquor. Actually, I couldn't smoke crack unless I had a drink of something strong. At one point, Orange Cisco, Night Train, Diamond Red, Mad Dog 20/20, Thunder Bird, Silver Satin, and Kool-Aid were my breakfast. I needed them in order to smoke crack. The only time I wasn't smoking crack was when I went to jail or prison. And every time I went to jail, death was on me. Somebody was out to kill me, but God made a way of escape! God said He will protect you and He did just that; it was nobody but Jesus! His mercy endures forever! I remember getting high with all kinds of demons and spirits. If you don't water them down, they will make you kill yourself!

Notes

_____
_____
_____
_____
_____
_____
_____
_____
_____
_____
_____
_____
_____

Chapter 18

Delusional

After so long, I felt like a dead man walking. I didn't see anything but sex, drugs, money and all types of evil. My days were just like night. I didn't see any light. It was all darkness! Every day for twenty years, I lived in Sodom and Gomorrah. It was very dangerous because nobody could be trusted. I had been shot with my own gun and left for dead; I was found naked with my motel room door wide open not knowing what took place the night before. Gang bangers busted my head in with a 40-ounce bottle. I was beat with a 2 by 4 and almost killed in a motel room by a gang banger for something I didn't do, but a hater had blamed me.

When you're in this kind of life, everything goes. People will snitch on you for a $5 dollar hit not knowing it could take your life! Everybody is all about self and will do whatever it takes to get the next hit! This ended up making me out to be a hell raiser. I gang banged, so I wasn't a punk in the streets. So when it came to scrapping or handling my business, "Oh, I did just that!"

I thank God for being my protector. It wasn't at all me, but it was God! Thank you, Jesus for having my back. I felt like I was in the pit of hell right here on earth.

Anyone who smokes cocaine will go to hell and back to get the next hit! Remember people, "Never, say, never." You may find yourself in a place where you will have to come to your senses and ask, "How in the hell did I get here?" It was God's love that brought me back. Sometimes, I look back over my life, and I think things over. I can truly say that I've been blessed. I have a testimony! I want you to know today, all that I have shared with you was inspired by the leading of the Holy Ghost. Oh and I am not ashamed of the gospel, for it is the power unto my salvation! And now I realize "why."

On Aug. 8, 1999, I would be enlisted in the Army of the Lord! So, I had to go through something in order to get me to something. I wouldn't change it for the world!

Notes

_____

_____

_____

_____

_____

_____

_____

_____

_____

Chapter 19

Snitches

So, I continued in my mess, which all together summed up to twenty years of my life. I was in bondage just like the Israelites. I wandered in the wilderness, going around and around and around. Everything I left in L.A., I brought to Victorville.

One day, I was walking and a police officer pulled up and called me by my name. "Stephanie!" I asked him, "How do you know my name?" "Doesn't matter. This isn't LA.; it's Victorville. You stand out like a swollen finger, and everybody's snitching on you. Here's the deal- if I see you on the streets anymore today, I'm taking you to jail."

That was very scary to me, so I had to watch my back for the rest of the day from this police officer, until the shift changed because I couldn't let him see me anymore on the streets. I remember August 8, 1999. I felt a dark cloud over me. I felt like I just didn't want to live anymore. As a matter of fact, I felt the spirit of death over me. I was very, very tired of being sick and tired.

Notes

Chapter 20

Didn't Want to Live Anymore

I had no more strength to live and all hope was gone. I felt death on me. On August 8, 1999, I cried out to God saying, "I'm so tired, Lord. Help me please." I cried myself into a deep sleep. I wanted to give up. I felt there wasn't enough hope left. I had tried everything, and I tried everybody. No one could help me. I was feeling real heavy laden, like a cloud was over my head. I found out after my deliverance that when it feels like a cloud is over you, God is walking with you.

On August 8, 1999, I walked outside my motel room; it looked really gloomy outside, like it was getting ready to storm. I didn't have the strength to hustle. I didn't want to catch a date, and I didn't want to do anything but cry out for help! Jeremiah 29:10-14 says, *"This is what the Lord says: 'When several years are completed for Babylon, I will come to you and fulfill my gracious promise to bring you back to this place. For I know the plans I have for you," declares the Lord," plans to prosper you and not to harm you, plans to give you hope and a future. Then you will call upon me and come and pray to me, and I will listen to you. You will seek me and find me when you seek me with all your heart. I will be found by* you,' declares the Lord, 'and will bring you back from captivity. I will gather you from all the nations and places where I have banished you,' declares the Lord," and will bring you back to the place from which I carried you into exile."

For some reason, no one came into my room that day when usually somebody was knocking on my door every ten minutes. So, I went outside to see if I could get a free meal from somebody. I was very hungry and weak. I didn't see anyone. It felt as if it were a dream or as if I were in a daze. Something just didn't seem right. I slowly walked across the street to an AM/PM Arco gas station. I had a friend who worked there named Shay, who used to get high every now and then. She looked at me and saw something was wrong. She nodded her head as to say 'get what you want,' so God provided once again! I made some nachos, got a drink and walked out with a nod saying 'thank you.' I cried all the way back to my room and went to sleep.

I woke up around 12:30-1:00am feeling real sorry for myself. I wanted to die. I had no more strength to live; all my hopes and dreams were gone. I got up and started to pray to God to help me. "Please. I just don't want to live anymore." I started to remember my mother prayed for me; it was her prayer that got me through. At that time, she was resting in peace. I felt like I had not a friend in the world and everybody hated me. So, my life flashed before me, and I remembered how Mama used to take us to church every Sunday. The bible says, *"Train up a child in the way they shall go and when they get older they shall not depart."* So, I thought, *'Well Lord, I am going to give this prayer all I have left.'*

Notes

Chapter 21

The Visitation

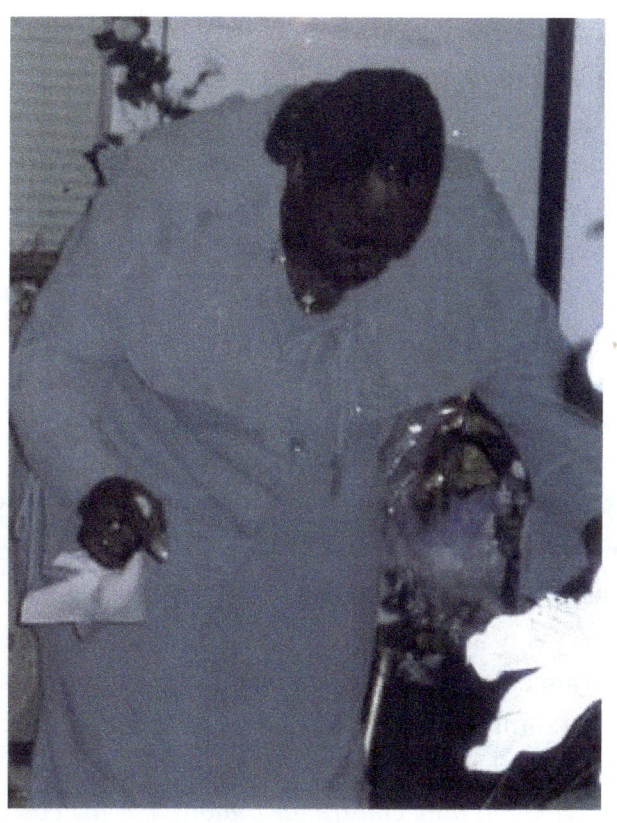

I got down on my knees and wept to my Lord and Savior. My exact words were, "I am going to try this one more time. Lord if, if, if there is a God, please come and see about me. Lord, I am tired. I am weary. I can't go on. I don't feel like going on. So, if there is a God, come please come, Lord and see about me!" Somewhere late in the midnight hour, God came and turned it around! When I woke up, the Shekinah Glory was in my room. It was so bright, I could hardly see. I began to leap and dance and jump and say, "Thank you, Jesus. Thank you, Jesus. Thank you, Jesus!"

Something had left my soul; the desire to smoke crack was gone! I had a new feeling of hope! God came in and replaced the craving of dope with the spirit of praise! I didn't have a hunger for crack! I had a hunger and thirst for righteousness. I had finally met this man name Jesus! While I was jumping around and thanking my savior, I heard a horn blow. I looked outside the window, and there were my guardian angels: Roz and Chubby. They were just coming to check on me. They had no idea Jesus was in the room when I opened the door. When I opened the door, they knew something was different. Something was new; something had happened. The back door was already open; I ran and jumped in the car, and said, "I am free. Let's go home!" Psalms 116 says, *"I love the Lord for he heard my cry."*

Every day after that, I couldn't stop talking about my deliverance. My mouth was going ninety miles per second telling about the goodness of the Lord and how the Lord had turned my midnight into day. The bible says, *"Weeping may endure for a night, but joy cometh in the morning."* I needed to get to a church, so I asked my sister what church they were going to, and she said, "We are not in church right now." I told her I had to find a church. I needed to go to church. I remember an old song that said, "Come and go with me to my father's house," and that's where I wanted to get to- my father's house. So, she told me there was a church up the street, and I asked them if they would drop me off there Sunday morning.

Notes

Chapter 22

Going to my Father's House

So, on Sunday morning, my sister dropped me off. I had an awesome time. For once, I felt like I was back to my original being. It didn't take long; God did a quick thing. I went back home and told my family what a good time I had. So the next Sunday, we all went and ended up joining the *Powerhouse of Deliverance Ministries* under Bishop Lola McGee.

I was baptized in the Holy Ghost with evidence of speaking in tongues. I worked as head usher and as the director of the praise team at one point. I worked with the youth drill team and choir; I wore many hats. I was just on the battlefield for my lord. I never wanted to get bored. I remembered to stay about my father's business. An idle mind is the devil's workshop! I didn't ever want to go back to my past life, so I kept busy. I went to *Power House* until Bishop passed away.

I then joined with two pastors that came out of *Powerhouse*: Carl and Juanita Ulmer at the *Temple of Praise*! Demetrius and I became their assistants. I came to find out that the battle was not mine, but it was truly the Lord's. I thank my lord and savior today that everything the devil meant for bad, God turned around for good. Today, I am a true believer that God can turn an impossible situation into a possible situation. That means God specializes in the impossibilities. He is a miracle-working god. Today, I am a miracle. I am an overcomer by the words of my testimony. I am more than a conqueror.

Notes

Chapter 23

Delivered

Today, as I ride around in my car, I hear the spirit of the Lord saying, "Do you see what I see?" I look around and the scales fall from my eyes and the spirit of the Lord falls upon me as things began to be revealed to me. The Lord spoke and said, "Do you remember when you were here?" I see sex, drugs, body piercings, tattoos, gang banging, fighting, homosexuality, lesbians, rape, torture, and idle minds. Basically, I see that the devil is still busy after all these years. There is a famine in the land. I would like to encourage you. If God did it for me, He can do it for you.

There is a man named Jesus, who is the Great Physician. At a set time, you will have an appointment with him. Amos 3:7 says, *"But always, first of all, I warn you through my servants the prophets. I, the Sovereign LORD, have now done this."* Joel 2:28 says, *"Then after I have poured out my rains again, I will pour out my spirit upon all people. Your sons and daughters will prophesy. Your old men will dream dreams. Your young men will see visions. In those days, I will pour out my spirit even on servants, men and women alike. I will cause wonders in the Heavens and on earth-blood and fire and pillars of* smoke. The sun will be turned into darkness, and the moon will be blood red before the great and terrible day of the Lord arrives. And anyone who calls on the name of the Lord will be saved. There will be people on mount Zion in Jerusalem who escape, just as the Lord has said. These will be among the survivors whom the Lord has called."

Notes

_____
_____
_____
_____
_____
_____
_____
_____
_____
_____
_____
_____

Chapter 24

More than a Conqueror

I can truly say that I am a survivor today. If you believe God, if you only believe God for your change, your change is here. In the twinkling of an eye, you will suddenly be changed. Somebody wants to come out; the spirit of God is saying, "How bad do you want it?" There's somebody going through something, struggling with something, addicted to something, bound by something, uncomfortable with something, tired of being sick and tired, needs to be delivered from something, something is bothering you, troubling you, ailing you, stressing you, or distracting you. It may be a sickness or death, not necessary a physical death but maybe a spiritual death. In order to live, something has got to die!

I want to let you know today the master Jesus Christ is still on the throne. He's the same yesterday, today, and forever more. I hope that if you are reading this book, you are being summoned into the king's palace for such a time as this. Somebody's coming out of bondage; somebody's going to get healed and set free! Somebody's going to break through; somebody's shackles are being let loose as you read this book!

If you know somebody that's addicted to drugs, alcohol, tattoos, body piercing, homosexuality, boys, girls, sex, lust, and pornography, then you must escort him/her to a man named Jesus who will set the person free from all hurt and pain. The bible says we are more than conquerors.

In order to be more than conquerors, there must be something to conquer or overcome. The bible says we are overcomers by the words of our testimonies. Today, we have some mighty, mighty women of God here in our society today to share their real life stories. Some have been molested all their lives, beaten all their lives, strung out on drugs, prostitutes and strippers. Some have experienced homosexuality, some are jackers, robbers, thieves, gangbangers, and this is what makes us S.W.A.T (Sisters with a Testimony). In order to have a testimony, you have to have a test. I come to let you know today it was only by the grace of God that I made it! I come to let you know there is hope! And it is time to bring it to Jesus- the healer, deliverer, the keeper, mind regulator, heart fixer, Jehovah Jireh the provider, battle fighter, the Good Shepherd, Jehovah Shalom, Prince of Peace, Jehovah Rohi.

Exodus 15:26 states, *"God spoke to me and said: it's not too late, take action go and compel my daughters and sons to return to their first love. For I am soon to return and I wish that no one would perish."* Today is a day of repentance and of forgiveness. The street lights are on; it's time for the back sliders to come home.

I came 'out of darkness' to 'God's marvelous light' from glory to glory.

It was a mind-blowing experience!

God has truly made a believer out of me!

I am an overcomer by the words of my testimony.

Notes

Definitions

Hustler- getting money by all means necessary (a go getter)

Pimp- womanizer, a man that has women who sell their bodies or steal and pay him the money and he in return takes care of them.

Prostitute- a woman who sells her body (has sex) in exchange for money

Mack- a smooth-talking man that talks based on facts with a lot of finesse (fact'n and mack'n)

Strawberry- a man or a woman that dates for dope.

Trick- a man that looks to buy sex from a prostitute. (Today, they get tricked instead of treated.)

Scandalous- a down low type of person who does anything to get a dollar or hit.

Wild 'N Out- out of control

Real Hoe- a woman that gets real money in a real way by stealing, pick pocketing, flat backing, oral sex, etc.

Serial Killer- someone that kills in a pattern or multiple people.

Free-base-cocaine- the original way of smoking which is melting down on the glass and scraping it; the first hit is free.

Game- just like it says (the game of life street version)

Pervert- someone that wants you to perform weird or strange sexual acts.

Date- sexual encounters with a male or female.

Scriptures from the New International Version of the Holy Bible

Proverbs 22:6- *"Start children off on the way they should go,*
and even when they are old they will not turn from it."

Ephesians 1:11- *"In him we were also chosen, having been predestined according to the plan of him who works out everything in conformity with the purpose of his will."*

Jeremiah 1:5- *"Before I formed you in the womb I knew you,*
before you were born I set you apart; I appointed you as a prophet to the nations."

Jeremiah 29:11-14- *"For I know the plans I have for you,"* declares the LORD, *"plans to prosper you and not to harm you, plans to give you hope and a future. ^{12} Then you will call on me and come and pray to me, and I will listen to you. ^{13} You will seek me and find me when you seek me with all your heart. ^{14} I will be found by you,"* declares the LORD, *"and will bring you back from captivity. I will gather you from all the nations and places where I have banished you,"* declares the LORD, *"and will bring you back to the place from which I carried you into exile."*

John 10:27-28- *"My sheep listen to my voice; I know them, and they follow me. ^{28} I give them eternal life, and they shall never perish; no one will snatch them out of my hand."*

Isaiah 40:31- *"But those who hope in the LORD will renew their strength. They will soar on wings like eagles; they will run and not grow weary, they will walk and not be faint."*

Psalm 139:13-14- *"For you created my inmost being; you knit me together in my mother's womb. ^{14} I praise you*

The Woman in the Now

because I am fearfully and wonderfully made; your works are wonderful, I know that full well."

Psalms 27- "The L{\sc ord} is my light and my salvation whom shall I fear? The L{\sc ord} is the stronghold of my life— of whom shall I be afraid? ² When the wicked advance against me to devour me, it is my enemies and my foes who will stumble and fall. ³ Though an army besiege me, my heart will not fear; though war break out against me, even then I will be confident. ⁴ One thing I ask from the L{\sc ord}, this only do I seek: that I may dwell in the house of the L{\sc ord} all the days of my life, to gaze on the beauty of the L{\sc ord} and to seek him in his temple. ⁵ For in the day of trouble he will keep me safe in his dwelling; he will hide me in the shelter of his sacred tent and set me high upon a rock. ⁶ Then my head will be exalted above the enemies who surround me; at his sacred tent I will sacrifice with shouts of joy; I will sing and make music to the L{\sc ord}. ⁷ Hear my voice when I call, L{\sc ord}; be merciful to me and answer me. ⁸ My heart says of you, "Seek his face!" Your face, L{\sc ord}, I will seek. ⁹ Do not hide your face from me, do not turn your servant away in anger; you have been my helper. Do not reject me or forsake me, God my Savior. ¹⁰ Though my father and mother forsake me, the L{\sc ord} will receive me. ¹¹ Teach me your way, L{\sc ord}; lead me in a straight path because of my oppressors. ¹² Do not turn me over to the desire of my foes, for false witnesses rise up against me, spouting malicious accusations. ¹³ I remain confident of this: I will see the goodness of the L{\sc ord} in the land of the living. ¹⁴ Wait for the L{\sc ord}; be strong and take heart and wait for the L{\sc ord}."

Psalms 23- "The L{\sc ord} is my shepherd, I lack nothing. ² He makes me lie down in green pastures, he leads me beside quiet waters, ³ he refreshes my soul. He guides me along the right paths for his name's sake. ⁴ Even though I walk through the darkest valley, I will fear no evil, for you are *with me; your rod and your staff, they comfort me. ⁵ You prepare a table before me in the presence of my enemies. You anoint my head with oil; my cup overflows. ⁶ Surely your goodness and love will follow me all the days of my life, and I will dwell in the house of the LORD forever."*

Psalms 121- *"I lift up my eyes to the mountains—where does my help come from? ² My help comes from the LORD, the Maker of heaven and earth. ³ He will not let your foot slip— he who watches over you will not slumber; ⁴ indeed, he who watches over Israel will neither slumber nor sleep. ⁵ The LORD watches over you— the LORD is your shade at your right hand; ⁶ the sun will not harm you by day, nor the moon by night. ⁷ The LORD will keep you from all harm—he will watch over your life; ⁸ the LORD will watch over your coming and going both now and forevermore."*

Romans 8:28- *"And we know that in all things God works for the good of those who love him, who have been called according to his purpose."*

Romans 8:38-39- *"For I am convinced that neither death nor life, neither angels nor demons, neither the present nor the future, nor any powers, ³⁹ neither height nor depth, nor anything else in all creation, will be able to separate us from the love of God that is in Christ Jesus our Lord."*

About the Author

Prophetess Stephanie Gamble was raised in Los Angeles, CA in a family of four brothers, three sisters, her God-fearing mother Sarah, and her caring father Edmore. She accepted Jesus at the age of seven years old. She attended Greater Ebenezer Baptist Church, then Mount Mariah Baptist Church, where she sang in the youth choir. Her parents divorced while she attended junior high school. After graduating from Locke High School (1979), she enrolled into Southwest Jr. College and majored in Fashion Merchandising (1980).

Prophetess Stephanie Gamble graduated from the school of hard knocks university! She earned a Ph.D. from the streets and is now serving with a B.A. (Born Again) degree from God Almighty! Prophetess Gamble was commissioned to go into the highways and the byways to tell her testimony of how God broke her loose of the shackles that had her bound. She was strung out on crack cocaine, and she was involved in prostitution for twenty years! Prophetess Gamble is one who flows in the prophetic gifting. She is anointed, appointed, and chosen by God to fulfill the call placed upon her life; she is saved, sanctified, and filled with His precious Holy Ghost to do the Master's will, as a humble servant. Evangelist Gamble is a living example of what God can and will do! She testifies strait laced, no chase. Her powerful, raw, uncut, unfiltered testimony about how God brought her from darkness (sex, sin, and drugs) to His Marvelous Light (Glory Glory) is life changing.

Prophetess Gamble came from

"Bondage to Break-Through"

From Trials to Triumphs

She quotes Amazing Grace!

How sweet the sound

That saved a wretch like me.

I once was lost

But now I am found

Was blind but now I see

The Holy Ghost in me!!!!

To God be the Glory!!!!

Hallelujah, now I'm free!!

A Message from the Author

I love the Lord for what He's done, and I worship Him for who He is. But most of all, I love the Lord because He heard my cry! God Bless!

Stay tuned for my second book: *Me and my Boaz: Back to Back!* A double portion of God's grace; what God has joined together let no man put asunder! To God be the glory introduces S.W.A.T Soul Winning Action Team: Soldiers with a Testimony. Mr. and Mrs. G's God's End Time Army.

One thing about me was I worked my hood. I lived off 65th and Figueroa, and I did all my street walking from Exposition to Imperial on Figueroa. This was one of the busiest boulevards for prostitution in the eighties and nineties. I stayed close to home. If something were to happen to me, my family would be the first to know. Me and my prostitute buddies were well known by all the dope spots.

I decree and declare, I am the women in the now.
I don't think the way I used to think!
I don't dress the way I used to dress.
I don't hang around mess; I hang around the women of God.
I used to dance for him (the devil), but now I dance for Jesus.
I don't walk the way I used to walk.
I don't talk the way I used to talk.

I don't walk in the counsel of the ungodly nor do I sit in the seat of the scornful.

But I do "delight" myself in the Lord, and He's been faithful to give me the "desires of my heart"!

I can't help but meditate day and night because nothing more gives me joy!

"To God be the glory." I was enlisted as a soldier in the army of the Lord on Aug. 8, 1999. Since then, I have been elevated to a general in God's (end time) army! I was bent over for 20 years just like the woman with the issue of blood, except my issues were crack cocaine and prostitution. When God came in the room, He asked, "Do you want to be made whole?" and I answered, "Yes." He said, "You are healed. Now go and sin no more." God has lifted my head. Thank you, Jesus for lifting my head. Just like Lazarus, God called and said, "Stephanie, come out. Take off the grave clothes and live." Today, I truly know that God saw the best in me when everyone else saw the worst in me. To God be the glory forever and ever. Amen.

Stay tuned for book two: *Me and My Boaz: Back to Back.*

www.ingramcontent.com/pod-product-compliance
Lightning Source LLC
Chambersburg PA
CBHW051706090426
42736CB00013B/2566